Improve your
management skills

Improve your management skills

JEAN CIVIL

WARD LOCK

To Irene Booth

A WARD LOCK BOOK

First published in the UK 1997
by Ward Lock
Wellington House
125 Strand
London
WC2 0BB

A Cassell Imprint

Distributed in the United States
by Sterling Publishing Co., Inc.
38 Park Avenue South, New York, NY 10016-8810

A British Library Cataloguing in Publication Data block for this book may be obtained from the British Library

ISBN 0 7063 7705 2

Designed, edited and produced by Pardoe Blacker Publishing Ltd, Lingfield, Surrey RH7 6BL

Printed in Hong Kong by Midas Printing Limited

CONTENTS

Chapter 3: How can I communicate more successfully with people?

Chapter 4: What do I do in meetings to achieve the results I want?

Acknowledgements

I would like to thank all the hundreds of managers I have met over the years as a Management Trainer, for their quotes, insights and stories. Hearing your stories made it possible for me to know and write about managers.

A special thank you to Jeannie Turnock for her computer skills in typing this book, and particularly for her excited interest and constant encouragement while I was writing it.

I am indebted to Norman Dickie, my co-trainer, for the witty – even rude – comments he made when he read the first drafts. He really helped me to focus.

I would also like to thank some great trainers with whom I have worked: Derek Marsh, Brenda Mallon, Colin Turner, Pablo Foster, Diane Brace and the late Bill Pasquerella, for all their expertise and insights and humour over the years of our management training.

Thanks go particularly to Mike Bryan, Ray Masters and the staff at Network Training; also to Salix Education for the use of my *Enjoy being assertive* brochure.

Then there are all the managers who have managed ME! In particular two terrific ones: Alan Chitty and Liz Balinger. I am so grateful to my agent Alan Gordon Walker who gave me confidence and made it all happen and the superb staff at Pardoe Blacker.

Finally, but really by no means least, to my son Carl who did some word processing and commented on the contents, and my husband Geoff, who supported me emotionally and physically throughout the months of continuous work involved.

INTRODUCTION

To be happy and feel successful in your working environment means you can get much more out of your life. It's a sobering thought that most people in full-time paid employment are likely to spend more of their life at work than at home, so it is vitally important to be joyful and able to succeed in your place of work.

Succeeding will mean different things to different people. Maybe you want to be more effective, or efficient, be retired, gain promotion, be better organized, make time for lunch breaks or try to do the things you should do at work instead of just the things you have to do. It could be that you feel under constant pressure and never able to complete tasks or step back enjoying a sense of achievement, for as soon as you start to work on any given job, another project or task looms ahead.

If your job involves dealing with people at all levels and for many different reasons, then possibly there are times when communications go wrong. You are surprised at people's response. Or you are constantly trying to deal with those who demand your time when you had planned to do something else. Even when it is part of your job to relate positively to

first time MANAGER

people, there may be times when you feel shattered by the many daily interactions and distractions.

Perhaps you are feeling overwhelmed with all the paper work, telephone calls, meetings or administrative duties that you have to manage.

Or you may feel pressurized by certain individuals or situations and be looking for ways to handle the pressure and improve your confidence and your assertiveness skills.

If you can identify with any of these thoughts, then this book is for you. It is intended to help you to organize your energies and thoughts in a way that will reward you at work, while at the same time having the beneficial side-effect of improving your home life.

In the book there are a mixture of questionnaires to enable you to focus on how you think or behave. From your answers you will gain insight into how to gain a more joyful and productive use of your time and, therefore, your life. The book also includes tips on how to deal with people, paper and pressure. Finally, it looks at how you can sell yourself at work by looking confident and behaving assertively.

CHAPTER 1

How can I decide which skills I need to improve?

The quickest and easiest way would be to ask members of your team, but this assumes that you have the kind of relationship that makes them honest enough to tell you. There may be many reasons why they would not tell you their real feelings: they may be in awe of you, envious, frustrated, angry or just want to please you. It is worth analyzing which members of your team would give you genuine and constructive feedback. Most managers would always be supported by 20 per cent of their staff, disliked by 20 per cent, with the remaining 60 per cent in the middle, swinging from one position to the other.

This book is designed to show you how to improve your management skills, which will help you to influence your staff. To start with, you need to recognize your present strengths and weaknesses. It is important to celebrate your successes as well as to mark the areas where you need improvement and training: if you cannot enthuse yourself, then it is going to be very difficult to enthuse others.

This chapter starts with four questionnaires so that you can focus on your own particular work issues. By first identifying these joy and time blockers, and celebrating what makes you happy at work, you will be able to elicit practical suggestions from the rest of the book.

QUESTIONNAIRE 1
Joy blockers

● ●

List below the ten things that most prevent you from feeling successful at work:

1 _____

2 _____

3 _____

4 _____

5 _____

6 _____

7 _____

8 _____

9 _____

10 _____

QUESTIONAIRE 2
Managing time

● ●

List below the ten things that most rob you of time on the job:

1	
2	
3	
4	
5	
6	
7	
8	
9	
10	

It is important to be clear whether the things that rob you of feeling successful, or of wasting your time at work, are about people, paper, or pressure.

So now try to analyze your answers to Questionnaires 1 and 2 by putting them into the following three areas:

People	Paper	Pressure

If you have a preponderance of people issues that prevent you from feeling successful or take up your time, then you will gain helpful ideas from the section on finding out whether you are passive, assertive or aggressive. This will help you to find better ways of trying to help people with their issues or concerns.

If you have blockers or time wasters in the paper column, you will benefit from the section on how to manage your time.

If the pressure column is the largest, then working on the section about dealing with pressure may help you.

Hopefully you will find something in all three areas to improve your level of joy and success at work.

Before you begin to open some doors, give thought to what you know you could do but perhaps don't. Then think about what makes you happy at work.

QUESTIONNAIRE 3
What could I do?

● ●

What could I do to save time when dealing with people, paper or pressure? Make a list of ten things that you already know you could do, but perhaps you don't.

1 _____

2 _____

3 _____

4 _____

5 _____

6 _____

7 _____

8 _____

9 _____

10 _____

QUESTIONNAIRE 4
Happiness is ...

• •

List ten things that make you feel happy at work.

Happiness is ...

1 _____
_____

2 _____
_____

3 _____
_____

4 _____
_____

5 _____
_____

6 _____
_____

7 _____
_____

8 _____
_____

9 _____
_____

10 _____
_____

Look down your list and tick the ones that have happened for you in the last month.

When you have read the book, return to the questionnaires on pp. 12–16 and see if you want to delete or add to any of your answers. This could be a measure of your progress.

I wonder what kind of impression I make at work?

You have no way of knowing what kind of impression you make at work unless you ask people. It is likely that you will make many different impressions according to who you ask and their perception of you. People will judge you by their own value systems.

Having succeeded in attaining your job, by knowing how to put together your CV in a way that is clear, concise and complementary to the position for which you have applied, you now actually have to do your job. How you set about doing it is, in the main, up to you, given the limitations of your systems and personnel.

How people perceive you is up to them, but also up to you. Their impression of you can be affected by the way you speak, behave or even dress. Let us take a look at how you dress.

People can be very subjective, prejudiced and stereotypical about you, especially on an initial meeting. If your job involves your travelling and meeting new people, you need to remember that 'you never get a second chance to make a first impression'. Many things can go wrong with the best-laid plans, so you may decide to avoid adding to these by being unsuitably attired. Of course, you can choose to dress how you want. You may think that is the other people's problem if they don't like it, and it is; but remember, we all have choices and with those choices come consequences. The consequences may mean that you don't get the job, contract, position, status, respect, promotion or influence you think you deserve. If any of these things make you feel successful, you may be losing out.

Some of the following statements are specifically aimed at either women or men, others at both sexes. Keeping in mind fashion changes for both genders, here are some comments made by an American tutor, Lisa Ford, at a conference I attended on how to empower yourself at work.

Supposedly, if you wear a jacket, 80 per cent of what you say is believed. Dark colours are more empowering than light colours. Light shirts with dark suits are positive. Dark shoes with dark socks for men, or stockings or tights for women, are more powerful. Open-toed shoes are negative – apparently, men are turned on by peep-toe shoes. Medium-heeled shoes are better than high-heeled ones, although fashions may change this. No make-up is as bad as too much make-up. Shoulder pads empower, although softer fashion is now more in vogue. Long earrings are 'credibility snatchers': apparently people will be watching the earrings swaying rather than listening to what is being said. Finally, briefcases. Large, bulging briefcases are less powerful than the thin document case. Possibly the reason for this is that it is assumed your personal assistant has put just the limited, correct amount of papers in it for your meeting, and that some people carry all sorts of rubbish in large brief-cases, including lunch, and never clean them out.

So, in terms of the impression you are making, maybe you need to think about one aspect of yourself: your appearance.

The next chapter looks at ways in which your behaviour might affect how people perceive you and whether your behaviour prevents you from succeeding or enjoying being at work.

CHAPTER 2

Does my behaviour prevent me from succeeding at work?

Now that you have started to learn what stops you from being successful and what or who tends to waste your time, let us look at you. How do you behave towards your staff? Before I go any further with explanations, complete the following questionnaire. The analysis will then make more sense.

If you read the analysis before you do the questionnaire, it will influence your answer. So don't cheat.

Remember there are no right or wrong answers. Be honest, avoid trying to give a good impression. You will only be fooling yourself.

Answer 'Yes' or 'No' to all of the following questions. Tick the appropriate boxes if you are wavering or thinking sometimes it is probably 'Yes'. Now turn to the questionnaire.

QUESTIONNAIRE 5
My behaviour

● ●

1 Do you try to conceal your feelings?   Yes ☐ No ☑

2 Are you reticent in asking others to help?   ☐ ☑

3 When setting standards for yourself are they usually too high?   ☐ ☑

4 Do you sometimes feel 'put upon' when helping others?   ☐ ☑

5 Do you take on too many jobs at the same time?   ☑ ☐

6 Do you dislike letting go of a job, thinking that with a bit more effort you could improve the result?   ☐ ☑

7 Do you like to get things right?   ☑ ☐

8 Do you like to be liked and prefer to be popular rather than unpopular?   ☑ ☐

9 Are you a better instigator than a finisher?   ☑ ☐

10 Do you try to fit in more jobs than you could realistically hope to complete?   ☑ ☐

11 Is it difficult for you to say no?   ☑ ☐

12 Do you tend to collect the coffee money and organize the leaving present or works party?   ☐ ☑

13 Do you find it difficult to delegate, even if you have someone you can rely on?   ☐ ☑

14 Do little things annoy you, such as a picture not quite straight on a wall, a disorderly desk, wallpaper peeling, spelling mistakes?   ☐ ☑

15 Do you become irritated when someone takes ages to come to the point? ☑ ☐

16 Do you find it difficult to use the word excellent? ☐ ☑

17 Do you use other people as a yardstick for your own performance and judge yourself accordingly? ☐ ☑

18 Are you reluctant to give up a job, even wanting to finish reading a book rather than be disturbed? ☐ ☑

19 Do you go to work when you are feeling ill even though others would stay away with the same symptoms? ☑ ☐

20 Do you finish people's sentences for them in the hope that they will get on with it? ☑ ☐

21 Do you like to keep things tidy at home or have your filing cabinet and desk in order? ☐ ☑

22 Do you hate people wasting time talking about what they might do instead of just getting on with it? ☐ ☐

23 Would you find it difficult to share your personal concerns with someone? ☐ ☑

24 Do you try to avoid conflict so as not to upset other people? ☑ ☐

25 Do you push yourself to achieve a better job or relationship or to gain more qualifications? ☐ ☑

How to score

Give yourself one mark for a 'Yes' and zero for a 'No' answer.

Now complete the following five columns, putting your score next to the question numbers. For example, for column A question 3, if you have answered 'Yes', give yourself 1 mark. If you have a 'No' answer, then put a zero.

COLUMN A	COLUMN B	COLUMN C	COLUMN D	COLUMN E
3	4	5	1	6
7	8	10	2	9
14	11	15	13	17
16	12	20	19	18
21	24	22	23	25
1	3	4	1	1

Now add up your score for each of the separate columns. You will have separate scores for columns A B C D and E.

Where you have a score of 3 or more in one column, it is likely that you exhibit that kind of behaviour. Now let us look at what the columns indicate.

Analysis

You may have come across the idea of creatures or monkeys sitting on your shoulders. These creatures give you internal messages, which create a dialogue between yourself and your creatures. They talk to you about how you should behave or what you should think. They were put on your shoulders when you were young. Whatever your childhood experiences were, either positive or negative, you were still given early behavioural messages: how to be careful when you crossed the road; what and how to eat; how to dress yourself. There are both positive and negative messages. Some would be positive and helpful like 'be happy' but other negative ones may have had long term damaging effects, like you're 'stupid', 'thick', 'no good at sports', 'can't draw', 'a nasty evil person', 'a waste of space' and so on.

As you have matured and been influenced by other factors and people, some of the creatures may have dropped off your shoulders. Nevertheless, let us have a look to see if they might still be chatting to you.

What do the columns tell you?

Column A	Be perfect
Column B	Please people
Column C	Hurry up
Column D	Be strong
Column E	Try harder

Management styles

You may have heard jokes about different kinds of managers:

Mushroom management – *keep staff in the dark. Every now and again throw a load of manure on to them.*

Kipper management – *two-faced and spineless.*

Goldfish management – *the dead rise to the top.*

Diamond room management – *the equivalent of the 'Be perfect' manager.*

Below we look more closely at these management styles and describe the key characteristics to help you identify them in the workplace.

The be perfect manager

The diamond room manager lives in a room full of diamonds; diamond ceiling, floor and walls. Yet right in the corner is a load of manure. Instead of seeing the diamonds around you, you focus on the manure. Similarly, you might find yourself concentrating on the small percentage of things that are wrong with an individual instead of celebrating the diamonds in their make-up.

You may play the psychological game of 'blemish', which again is looking for the mistake rather than appreciating the whole. For instance, someone hands you a finished project and your first reaction is 'There's a spelling mistake on page 90' instead of saying 'Thank you there's a lot of good work gone into this. However I am concerned about one or two small spelling mistakes, so let's get those right.'

You work at 100 per cent; 80 per cent is not good enough. You drive yourself to do everything to perfection. Whether it is how you dress, the way you keep your desk, or how you submit papers and reports.

You create a lot of stress for yourself by wanting to be perfect all the time. Probably you try different skills – hobbies even – you become proficient at something but because you cannot get it perfect you drop that and try something else. You constantly think that you could have done it better.

If someone says to you 'Well done, I'm really pleased with this report, it's excellent', you don't believe them. You are convinced that you could have done it better if you had had more time – added flow charts, illustrations, cartoons, improved the layout or the binding. Besides that, you don't use the word excellent, for nothing in your view is ever excellent; there is always room for improvement.

You are a pain to work with. Some of your staff may find you really difficult to work with. As they are human it is virtually impossible for them to work at 100 per cent – even on good days it is impressive if people operate at 80 per cent, at which point they will still be effective. Perhaps you are remiss about praising them because you are always looking for perfection. On the other hand, sometimes you might be quite full of praise for your staff but very hard on yourself. Try asking your staff for feedback.

The pleasing people manager

If you are this kind of manager, then you will probably nod a lot and smile a lot at people. Even when you don't agree or feel upset. Remember, powerful people smile when pleased, powerless people smile to please. You only need to smile

when you want to, otherwise your staff will never really know when you are genuinely pleased with them.

You are likely to be anxious about being pleasant to people, do not want to hurt their feelings and try to say supportive things to your team. You will often be the one who thinks about the collection for someone's present, organizes the works Christmas party, or sends the flowers and so on.

You are probably liked, but may come over as pretty ineffectual when it comes to sorting out conflict issues. Managers who want to please others usually have great difficulty in sorting out and managing conflict.

When you were small you were likely to have been told to think about what the neighbours would say, how it was important to be nice to people. The message that you were picking up then was that unless you were pleasant to people you were no good. Somehow you would be punished, so your style is to make others feel good so that you can feel better.

Let me give you an example of a childhood that leads to pleasing people behaviour. You may not have any children, in which case think about your own childhood or that of other children you know. If you do have children, especially two with less than four years between them, think about how you have influenced them.

Scenario: The mother of a four-year-old is now pregnant and explains to her child: 'Mummy and Daddy love you very much, we love you so much that we are going to have another one just like you.' Imagine your partner saying that to you: 'I love you very much, so I'm going to have another one just like you.' How would you feel? Pretty upset I would imagine. Unless of course you want to finish the relationship, then you would probably feel a sense of relief.

Yet this is what can happen at work, especially from managers who want to please their staff by being pleasant, or who want to please their own line manager even when turned down for promotion. They find it difficult to give the bad news. 'You know we think you are a really good worker, it was so difficult to choose, but eventually after much soul-searching we gave the job to the other person.'

Great; if they thought that much about you how is it that the other candidate got the job? They might even add, 'The other person can't start for two months, so we would like you to do the job until they arrive, sorry there is no extra pay, and then perhaps you could show them how to do the job when they arrive for their new post.' Has something similar ever happened to you? Or have you said that kind of thing to some of your staff? Poor management, I'm sure you would agree. Yet it is happening all the time.

Anyway, back to the scenario. The baby is born and the four-year-old is terribly nice, doing all the things modern parents require: being very pleasant to the new baby but underneath wishing its mother would send it back where it came from and love her again like she used to. How about work, have you had your nose pushed out of joint by some new, younger protégé? Do you wish it was like it was before with a particular line manager or member of staff that you manage?

If you have a pleasing people creature on your shoulder, you will have to learn how to deal with conflict situations, how to give the bad news and also how to say 'No'. Your staff are more likely to know where they stand if you occasionally display your displeasure.

The hurry up manager

Everything is such a rush for you. You are always busy doing so many things simultaneously, hurrying here, hurrying there, but still thinking about what else you ought to be doing instead. When you are in a meeting, you think about who you need to speak to at lunch and after work. When you are at lunch, you are thinking about being back in the meeting. You

probably tap your fingers or twitch your leg more than most. Your speed is admirable, but how are your staff affected? They try to stop you in the corridor but you are in a hurry; 'I'll see you later' is your reply, but 'later' you're just as busy.

You probably take on too many things. You offer yourself for committees, agree to give people lifts in your car, but then hold them up because you have to finish something vital before you leave. Your staff are probably worn out trying to keep up with your never-ending energy and new ideas; they wish that you would finish one job before shooting off to do something else.

It is likely that you arrive late for meetings, letting everyone know how busy you've been and how someone just stopped you with something really important. If, by accident rather than design, you arrive early, you will make a couple of telephone calls to fill the time. After all, you hate wasting time.

You are likely to be a 'stresser'. That is that you give people stress but may not suffer from it yourself. Well, you haven't got the time, have you? Now can you get off your hamster wheel for a while and slow down. Your staff would most likely appreciate some uninterrupted time with you without your feeling compelled to answer the telephone, just have a quick word with someone, or complete something in time for the post. In fact you are probably reading or skimming this book because really you think you ought perhaps to be doing something else. Give your staff a break, relax.

The be strong manager

Well, aren't you the Goody Two-Shoes? You never, or hardly ever, have time off work. Go in even when you are ill, while others are off sick with the same condition. You're there, rain

or shine, in sickness and in health, never recognizing when you're tired or hungry, just keeping going. You wait until the weekend or holidays to be ill.

Being strong has its positive side for you as a manager, for you are able to cope, are reliable, take on more work, never ask for help. Consider, however, the effect of your behaviour on your staff. You probably do not delegate for two reasons:

1   You would have to keep checking up on them all the time, so you might as well do it yourself in the first place.

2   If you did delegate, that member of staff might do it better than you and you would not like that would you? No one to delegate to, is that what you are thinking? Probably not – after all who would come up to your standards. But even if there were staff to whom you could delegate, you would still play 'martyr.'

It is important to be trusting, showing our vulnerable side to colleagues. Not you, you cope alone. You don't believe in airing your dirty linen in public. If that's what you believe, fine; but be aware of the consequences of that option. All options have consequences.

This may not be like you, but consider this scenario. Someone is betrayed or rejected by a partner. They feel angry and hurt so they decide to put up a shield in order not to be hurt again. The shield protects them from the hurt coming in but it also stops love coming in and prevents the anger from getting out.

Whatever your reasons are for wanting to be strong, recognize how that behaviour may affect you in an appraisal interview. When asked 'Do you need any support in your job?' you know the answer before you've read the question; no, you're fine.

The message that you give out to staff may be 'don't come to me with your problems, I am wonder-woman or superman' or, 'I can cope and so should you'. Can you recognize these characteristics in yourself: there early, staying late, looking towards the car park to check if you are working longer than others. Have you no home to go to? But then if you did have personal problems you would not disclose them at work would you, what would people think? It takes a very strong manager to show their vulnerable side, and it also means that most people can relate to you more easily if they think you are simply human.

The try harder manager

If you have found that your internal dialogue is about trying harder, you are likely always to be searching for something else. Just take stock of what is good about this job, this relationship. Ask yourself, who are you trying harder for? Or if you prefer, 'for whom are you trying harder?'

As a manager, you probably keep pushing yourself to get better results, more productivity, higher profit margins, better staff, quicker service, improved quality. Good, but what about you and your team?

Are they also expected to do more and more without reward? Do you set standards and targets that are difficult to attain?

Just because you are ambitious and never satisfied, please accept that some staff may not share your constant ambition to drive forward without recognizing the positive aspects of the workplace or workforce.

Scenario: you come home from school and say, excitedly, 'I came second at maths!' 'Who came first?' is the reply. Recognize that reply as one that means you must always be trying harder.

Final analysis

Refer back to the score sheet on page 22. You have now read detailed descriptions of the different styles of management. If you had a low score in one column (Be perfect) this does not necessarily mean that you do not get things perfect. You are still aiming for perfection, but you are choosing to get things perfect, rather than listening to your inner voice, which is saying: 'unless you get this perfect, you are worthless'. This applies also to the other four categories: pleasing because you want to, hurrying when necessary, being strong to support and trying harder to improve standards.

Having worked through these possible management behaviours, can you think of any colleagues that meet these descriptions? Remember the health warning: you are not just this, you are many-faceted.

Put in their names then check with them to see if they agree with you. It could make for an interesting discussion.

Be perfect	Please people	Hurry up	Be strong	Try harder

Finally, as well as sharing values with some of your staff you may be sharing behaviour. Do you get on better with people that behave as you do?

Having identified the 'inner invisible manager' who manages you, what can you do about it?

■ If you are into being perfect then, when all else fails, lower your standards. You will hate this as a solution.

■ Instead of pleasing others learn to love yourself. You don't need other people's approval before you can approve of yourself. When people reject you, you don't have to reject yourself.

■ Hurrying up all the time is stressful for you and others: slow down, take some 'selfish' time for yourself.

■ Being strong is good but not if it means that you turn your feelings in on yourself and then get depressed. Leave others to look after themselves. Look after yourself and be prepared to say, 'I need some support.'

■ By trying harder you may be missing out on the good things of today, always thinking of the future and feeling unhappy because if only you worked better life would improve. Enjoy the now, celebrate your current success.

CHAPTER **3**

How can I communicate more successfully with people?

Transactional Analysis

In order to feel a sense of achievement and success in your working day, you will need to feel that you have related to colleagues positively, but sometimes you may feel confused because communication somehow went wrong. Your intentions were good and you did not expect the response you received. So what went wrong? How can you relate to people more productively?

There are many reasons why communications can go wrong. One could be that you have different motives from those of your staff. There may be hidden agendas, or it may be simply the way you say something or the language you use. Let us look at one model which explains how people may be communicating. This model is called Transactional Analysis (T.A.), originated by Eric Berne. It offers an explanation of what can happen when you think you are relating in one way but the other person hears your comment differently. Or if, in Transactional Analysis terms, you are 'coming from a different ego state'.

Berne originated the idea that we all have several 'ego states' from which we operate when conversing with people. He called these ego states Parent, Adult and Child.

His model followed the terminology of Sigmund Freud, the famous psychologist, and the idea that, like an iceberg, much of our personality is concealed below the surface, in our sub-conscious, which we keep well away from public view (see Diagram 1)

The aim of T.A. is to help you understand what you are *really* saying, and to comprehend what people *really mean* when they are talking to you. We often use a code to conceal our real feelings – the area that is below the waterline of the iceberg. The examples and illustrations that follow are designed to prepare you for the time when you do not get the response that you want, and to guide you as to what is *really meant* rather than what is *merely said*.

Diagram 1

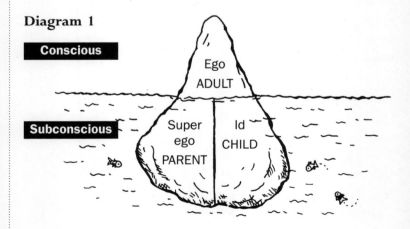

The ego states

Diagram 2

P	Parent adult ego states
A	Adult ego states
C	Child ego states

'You should be more thorough.' (summary of values, attitudes, judgemented, moralizing, punitive, directive)

Critical parent

Nurturing parent

'Mind how you go, take care.' (protective, caring, supportive, concerned, helpful, sympathetic)

Adult

'We have eight. Will that be enough?' (objective processing of information, rational part of self)

Little professor

Adapted child

Spontaneous child

'I've got a hunch!' (natural wisdom, intuitive, manipulative)

'If I'm very good will you love me?' (compliant, conforming, adapts to authority, apologetic, procrastinating)

'Let's have some fun!' (natural, spontaneous, open, aggressive, self-centred, sensuous, affectionate)

Facets of the ego states

Critical parent	
Words used	should, always, never, bad, ought, stupid, ridiculous, don't, everybody, no
Voice	critical, condescending, disgusted, sneering, authoritative, domineering, directive, ordering
Facial expression	frowning, scowling, hostile, rigid
Gestures, posture	arms folded, pointing finger, tapping feet, shaking head, lips tight, closed up

Nurturing parent	
Words used	let me, beautiful, nice, tender, don't worry, I care
Voice	concerned, loving, encouraging, sympathetic, supportive, understanding, protective, helpful
Facial expression	smiling, nodding, proud, loving, accepting
Gestures, posture	pat on back, caressing, relaxed, open arms

Adult	
Words used	where, what, when, facts, who, why, alternatives, results, reasons, check it
Voice	even, confident, enquiring, calm, decisive, unemotional
Facial expression	alert, open, thoughtful, attentive responsive, mischievous
Gestures, posture	erect, open, level

Adapted child	
Words used	can't, I wish, I'll try, please, thank you, sorry, help me
Voice	defiant, whining, sullen, servile, manipulating
Facial expression	pouting, sad, helpless, eyes downcast
Gestures, posture	dejected, curled up, still

Little professor	
Words used	why, who, where, when, what, how, ah, I've got an idea/a hunch
Voice	persuading, enthusiastic, can be manipulating
Facial expression	excited, alert, involved, dreamy
Gestures, posture	eyes alert, watching, listening attentively

Spontaneous child	
Words used	I want, mine, won't, I love, fantastic, fun, scared
Voice	loud, energetic, giggling, swearing, excited, playful, rebellious, aggressive
facial expression	relaxed, alive, wide-eyed, angry, joyful, seductive, curious
Gestures, posture	spontaneous, uninhibited, fidgety, lively

People do not necessarily remain in one state all the time although they may tend to use one state more often than another.

Successful communication depends on being able to:

1 RECOGNISE the type of behaviour
2 RESPOND in a way that enables communication to flow freely

How can I improve my responses?

Sometimes you may be operating from your adult state and asking for information, but your member of staff hears you asking from your 'critical parent'.

For example:
Manager: (Adult state)
'When will you return the finished project to me?'

Colleague: (hears the question from the manager's critical parent ego state and responds from their adapted child ego state)

'I don't know, I've got such a lot of work to do at the moment, I can't seem to get things finished. I'm ever so sorry.'

You need to be able to recognize this behavioural response in a way that enables communication to flow freely and respond with flexibility.

Let us consider different ways in which you may respond and try to identify the ego states in which you are operating.

'Its no good being sorry, I need it now. You have had ample time to get this finished.' (Critical parent)

'Yes I know how hard you have been working. Well, just see if you can get around to it soon but look after yourself, you are looking very tired these days.' (Nurturing parent)

'I recognize you need to prioritize: can you give me a time when you will bring the project to me?' (Adult)

'Oh I feel all work and no play is no good for either of us, let's go out at lunchtime and have a drink together.' (Spontaneous child)

You may think that there is a 'preferred response'. While people have the ability to work from all their ego states they probably have a preferred state. Some of your staff may be very critical and they probably get on with those who are themselves critical. Others may relate more frequently from their 'spontaneous child' and work well with you if that is your preferred state.

Now see if you can recognize the different ego responses to the manager's request in the following example:

Manager:

'I don't want you to continue with that job, I now want you to work on this project because it is a priority.'

Colleague:

Response 1: *'You are always changing your mind. I wish you would let me finish one thing before moving on ...'*

Response 2: *'Right, explain to me what exactly you need me to do ...'*

Response 3: *'Great! I could do with a change. So go on, this sounds exciting.'*

The first response is from a Critical parent, the second from the Adult and the third from the Spontaneous child.

Keep in mind the different transactions that you have with your staff. Point out when their response is not helpful, or when it sounds critical to you.

I forget conversations

A further reason for communications going wrong can be that you forget some of the conversations you have had.

There can be numerous reasons for your forgetting what people have said to you. Maybe you are preoccupied, or uneasy in their presence. Or maybe you are concerned about being perfect, pleasing people, hurrying up, being strong or trying harder. These behaviours may influence how much you tend to remember about what people have said to you.

If you are concentrating on getting the dialogue absolutely perfect, then you are unlikely to remember everything precisely. So sum up at the end of a discussion.

Of course, if you have been trying to please the other person, you were probably too busy thinking about smiling and nodding actually to listen to what they were saying, so extend yourself to the person who is talking, rather than thinking about how pleasant you are looking and if you are making them feel liked.

The most likely reason for forgetting what someone has said is probably the fact that you were in a hurry. So many things on your mind that you didn't really listen to what was said to you. You were busy thinking about what you had to do next, rather than what was happening to you at the time. So slow down, state how long you have got to listen and then check out what you have heard.

By being strong you may find that you expect too much of yourself. When someone has said something to you, you probably avoid saying that you don't understand, or you have forgotten their initial request. It is difficult for you to show your weaknesses, so try saying, 'Sorry, I forgot what you asked', or even 'I wasn't really listening to you'.

If your particular behaviour is to try harder, then however much you have remembered you will still think that you have forgotten something. So celebrate what you remember rather than what you have forgotten.

Supposedly, if we repeat or use any new information that we have been given within twenty-four hours, that knowledge is stored in the deep-memory box. So if someone asks you to do something, try to repeat it to someone else fairly quickly or respond to the request as quickly as possible. Acting on a conversation will help you to retain the information. If all else fails, you could resort to jotting down target points in your diary or using a mobile dictaphone to jog your memory.

As a checklist note that WE REMEMBER

10%	of what we read
20%	of what we hear
30%	of what we see
50%	of what we see and hear
80%	of what we say
90%	of what we say at the same time as we do it

So try talking to people and DOING IT, rather than using e-Mail or sending memos. There is then more chance of you remembering conversations, incidents and resolutions.

Why two-way communication fails in organizations

■ Poor relationships

■ Values are not shared

■ Upward communication is not encouraged by line managers or organization

■ Imbalance of the importance of messages sent down with those sent up

■ Emotions getting in the way

■ Status inhibiting staff from speaking up

■ Staff are not empowered

■ Physical barriers, noise or room-setting

■ Perceptual barriers based on rumour or fear

■ Poor listening skills

Some people take up so much of my time it is difficult to succeed

In order to feel at ease with people and spend an appropriate amount of time with them, it may be helpful for you to think about the following ways in which we may structure and allocate our time with people. By knowing this you may be able to recognize with whom you want to spend more or less time.

Many authors have added to Eric Berne's original model of T.A., in particular, Thomas A. Harris (*I'm OK You're OK.* 1967) and Claude M. Steiner (*Scripts People Live.* 1974). Berne offered the idea that we structure our time through several experiences. He wrote that, ideally, we need to be what he termed 'intimate' with people if we really want to achieve an honest, genuine relationship, but there are many steps of 'ritual sniffing' before we can get to that stage. Being intimate is game-free. Did you know that it is highly likely that you spend a lot of your time at work playing psychological games?

Berne suggests that when we meet people we structure our time according to how intimate we wish to be. He names these stages:

▶	Withdrawal
▶	Rituals
▶	Pastimes
▶	Activities
▶	Games
▶	Intimacy

Withdrawal

This may be either a physical or a psychological response. You may withdraw from certain groups or refuse a meeting. You may feel the need for time to reflect or find some quiet space from the noise and hubbub of the office, shopfloor or shared working area. Maybe you are withdrawing to avoid some conflict that is taking place between other people or between yourself and a colleague, client or line manager.

Psychologically you may withdraw from people even though you are physically present, say in a meeting or a group discussion. Perhaps you are bored or feeling emotional, either negatively or positively, about some remark that has been made. If you are withdrawing because you are angry, try to avoid turning your anger inwards, since this can lead to depression. Try to remember that depression can be a blanket over anger.

Rituals

Thomas Harris explains that a ritual is a socially programmed use of time in which everybody agrees to do the same thing. It is safe, and there is no commitment to, or involvement with, other people. The outcome is predictable. The ritual is designed to get a group of people through the hour without having to get too close to anyone. There is little commitment and therefore little fulfilment. Rituals, like withdrawal, can keep us apart.

For example, you may meet someone at work and this ritual conversation takes place:

You: *Good morning*

Reply: *Good morning*

You: *How are you?*

Reply: *Fine*

However, you may intend just to take part in a ritual but things may change. For example

You: *Good morning*

Reply: *Good morning*

You: *How are you?*

Reply: *Terrible! I've had a dreadful night. I've had this awful news about my friend who's been in an accident, and then this morning my cat died.*

While you only intended a ritual greeting, the other person changed the experience into something more intimate.

Activity

An activity, according to Eric Berne, is a 'common, convenient, comfortable and utilitarian method of structuring time'. For example, keeping business appointments, updating a filing system or correlating papers for the completion of a project. These activities, in that they may be creative and productive, can be highly satisfying, but during the time of the activity there is no need for any intimate involvement with any other person. There may be, but there does not have to be. Activities, like withdrawal and rituals, can keep us apart.

Pastimes

Pastimes are a way of passing time. Eric Berne defines a pastime as, 'an engagement in which the transactions are straightforward'. A social pastime may be indulged in for its own sake and bring satisfaction. Pastimes form the basis for the selection of acquaintances that may lead to friendship. Berne gives some names for these pastimes such as 'Small talk';

'General Motors' (comparing cars); 'How to' (go about doing something); 'How much?' (does it cost); 'Ever been?' (to some place); 'Do you know' (someone).

You: *I haven't seen you for years.*

Reply: *I know it must be six years since we worked together.*

You: *Are you still working there?*

Reply: *Yes, but a lot of people have left that you knew.*

You: *Is so-and-so still there?*

Reply: *Yes, and do you remember …*

■ Games

Games are so significant in transactions between people that Berne devoted a complete book to the games people play.

Games are time-consuming. They usually cause trouble. Thomas Harris explains that they are relationship wreckers and misery producers. The word 'game' does not necessarily imply fun or even enjoyment. A game is an on-going series of complementary ulterior transactions progressing to a well-defined, predictable outcome, often repetitious, superficial and plausible, with a concealed motivation.

Games are clearly different from rituals and pastimes in two ways: one, they have an ulterior aim or hidden agenda, and two, they have a pay-off which gives the game-player a chance to get into their bad feelings. Rituals can be effective, pastimes can be profitable, they may involve contest but not conflict, and the ending may be sensational, but not dramatic.

To quote Harris: 'Every game, on the other hand, is basically dishonest and the outcome has a dramatic, as distinct from merely exciting, quality.'

The names of games can be funny, but the games are not funny. Knowing what game you are playing does not necessarily make it possible for you to change. So decide on how much time you want to spend with people from whom you tend to withdraw and with whom would you like to be intimate. Ask yourself who plays psychological games with you. Games like:

Ain't it awful 'ere?

You: *Have the candidates arrived for the interview?*

Reply: *Yes, although I cannot believe anyone would want a job here.*

You: *If you could show them the interview room now, as we are running on a tight schedule.*

Reply: *I know, ain't it awful 'ere, there's no time for anything, and it's getting worse with this new management regime.*

Look at what you've made me do now

You: *Would you like to take your lunch break now?*

Reply: *I wish you wouldn't interrupt me when I'm working.*

You: *I really think you need to take a break.*

Reply: *Look what you've made me do now! I've just pressed the wrong button and lost all this morning's work off the computer screen because of your interruption.*

The blame game.

You: *How are you enjoying the new flexi-time?*

Reply: *I think they shouldn't meddle with a perfectly good system.*

You: *We'll soon get used to it, I'm sure, and it's lovely to have Friday afternoons off.*

Reply: *You may get used to it, but ever since it started I've been expected to do more hospital visits in the afternoon, which I absolutely hate. I blame the management. They don't seem to know what they want. This is just the flavour of the month.*

Poor me!

You: *I need you to change rooms, I realize that this will create a temporary disturbance for you.*

Reply: *Poor me! I've moved once this year already, I can't find the keys to the stock cupboard and now I've just had a phone call to say my cat's died.*

You: *Oh, I'm sorry about that. You must be upset.*

Reply: *I am. But then, everything goes wrong for me in my life, it doesn't matter what I try to do, nothing ever works out.*

Wooden leg

You: *Have you seen the new manager who's started today?*

Reply: *No, not yet, and I don't really want to.*

You: *She seems quite nice.*

Reply: *I applied for that job and I should have got it. If it hadn't have been for the fact that I couldn't go to university because I stayed at home to look after my mother, then it would have been a push-over. I never had her chances.*

What if

You: *What time is the full staff meeting being held this afternoon?*

Reply: *It's at two o'clock. I bet it's about redundancies.*

You: *We don't know that, yet, those may only be rumours.*

Reply: *What if it's true, and we all lose our jobs. I'll be first out because I was last in, and I need the money more than other people.*

Why don't you ... yes, but ...

You: *Why don't you establish a lunchtime rota for the telephone?*

Reply: *Yes, but then people wouldn't be able to organize their shopping or meeting other colleagues.*

You: *If you liaise with the staff, perhaps you could give them some choice.*

Reply: *Yes, but they'll all want different things and we won't be able to satisfy anybody.*

NIGYYSOB (Now I've got you, you son of a bitch)

You: *Hello! Did you want to see me?*

Reply: *Yes. Where is your answer to my memo about the salary figures?*

You: *I thought I had returned it.*

Reply: *Every time I send you a memo you ignore it. Last month you didn't give me the list of personnel, and six months ago you overlooked the expenses claim. And a year ago...*

This game is like NIGTTLAY (Now I'm going to throw the lot at you...).

Many games are played which are self-explanatory in their titles, for instance, 'Let you and the other person fight'. You can make up your own titles for the games played in your organization – the names are funny, but the games are not.

The golden rule is DON'T COLLABORATE with the game, remember that once you hit the ball back you are in the other person's game. Address the games by saying 'That sounds as if you are playing the "blame" game'.

■ Intimacy

This refers to an emotional intimacy which is game-free. If you are relating positively to someone, helping or counselling them, you need intimacy.

Intimacy is hard to explain, but it is mainly real, direct, open and honest interactions with people. Intimacy is gained through being in Thomas Harris's *I'm OK you're OK* state. Above all, intimacy can be described as being game-free. Ideally, you need to be game-free in all your relationships, but I guess few people are.

If you have only one hour to spend with someone, then learn about the Parent, Adult, Child ego states and how transactions work. This will be more useful to you than spending time on analyzing the reasons for their games.

In order to avoid people wasting your time, try recognizing the stages described and perhaps decide to stop colluding with their games. If you want real joy and success at work, move towards being intimate with a few chosen colleagues and be game-free with them.

Also, try some humour: nowadays humour and laughter are recognized by healers as a way of helping people. Humorous videos, cartoons and the sound of laughter can relieve certain types of stress. Sharing humour with your colleagues is likely to make you feel more positive about yourself and others. So try to make light of things. Laughing together unites people, which creates intimacy, and it is one of the better ways in which to feel happy and successful at work.

As a manager, you may be close to some of your staff. If so, you will be managing them more effectively than those with whom you play games or who play games with you. Aim to be honest, direct and game-free.

CHAPTER **4**

What do I do in meetings to achieve the results I want?

Now that you are a first-time manager you will need to consider the effect that you have on your staff when running meetings.

What has been your experience in meetings? How many times have you come out of a meeting and thought 'What a waste of time'? Well, what did you do about it?

Did you sit there and not say anything? Did you get angry and speak your mind regardless of how others were feeling, or were you offensive in your language about absent or previous colleagues?

All of these situations do not help to create harmony or achieve the results you want from your meeting.

What makes a good meeting?

Think of and write down one or two words that capture the experience of good meetings that you have attended

---

What makes a bad meeting?

Think of one or two words that describe a bad meeting for you.

The following lists show the shared responses (over 50 per cent) taken from 750 managers on my management training courses.

You will see that there were far more negative responses and feelings than positive experiences.

Shared responses to the following questions:		
What happened to make a good meeting for you?	What happened to make a bad meeting?	
Enjoyed challenges	People lied	Bad seating
A skilled chairperson	Too long	Competitive
Well organized	Dominated	Red herrings
Friendly atmosphere	Presence of certain	Game-playing
Open discussions	colleagues	Boring
Succinct language	No outcomes	Aggression
Tight agendas	Tension	No refreshments
Relevant discussions	Felt stupid	Had to take own
Generated good ideas	Humiliated	minutes
Felt good	Felt disliked	Felt frustrated
Felt involved	No structure	afterwards
Refreshments served	Dishonesty	Hidden agendas
Decisions made	Lack of trust	
Sense of achievement	Lack of recognition	
Well timed	Fear of redundancies	
Was productive	Repetitive	
Feelings were addressed	Tantrums	
	Offensive language	
	Disorganized	

Are there different types of meeting?

Yes. Although you are now a manager, I guess you can think of many different kinds of meetings that you have attended. Even though you may be involved in quick, high-powered decision meetings at work, at home some informal social meeting can take forever. Meetings can be fun or drudgery. They can be something you look forward to, or something that you dread. You may have fun with certain people or in some of the meetings that you attend.

However, if the mere thought of a meeting brings on that sinking feeling, it could well be that the people involved may adversely affect you, or maybe the way in which the meeting is managed causes you irritation. Or maybe you feel powerless because you are just being talked at, and think it is rather pointless being there at all, since your opinion is never sought.

It may seem like a 'when I want your opinion I'll tell you what it is!' type of meeting.

There are indeed different kinds of meetings, not necessarily good or bad, but with fancy titles that indicate their purpose and tell you what to expect.

The trouble is that many first-time and long-time managers don't know what type of meeting they are running, let alone how to run them.

So how skilled are you as a manager of meetings? Are you, or do you know of, managers who are unskilled at recognizing the basic human needs of other people attending the meeting? Unskilled in the art of listening, seeing, thinking, questioning or checking out hidden agendas?

If this last example is the sort of meeting that you hold most often, it would indicate that you are running an INFORMATION GIVING MEETING, that is the 'just listen and then go and do it' approach. This is a one-way communication process and not a good idea if you are hoping for commitment from your staff.

Then there are meetings that you are obliged to attend simply because it is Wednesday and you always have a meeting on a Wednesday at 11.00 a.m. These meetings go ahead regardless of whether there is anything to discuss, or important enough to take several people away from their work. This would be a COMMAND MEETING, where you are told, or tell others, to be present, maybe because of your status, role or job responsibilities. Again, this is often a one-way communication. Another kind of meeting is the COMMITTEE MEETING where people are representing their own interests or those of other people. They may be elected representatives, in which event it is essential and important that some formal minutes are taken as they are there on behalf of others.

I guess you have experienced getting together with your colleagues and having lots to talk about because you have so much work in common. This would be a COLLEGIATE MEETING where everyone is equal in status and all are perceived as being necessary to the success of the meeting. You sit down and work out a solution, given equal power and equal responsibility.

Now what about those difficult meetings when there is 'trouble afoot'? There may be two sides or a conflict of interest, perhaps dissent between management and staff, or between colleagues about pay, redundancies, or organizational change. This would be a NEGOTIATING MEETING where one wants 'x', another 'y' and you end up with 'z', often reaching an agreement that neither side wants. It is, therefore, important that any agreed outcome is written down. In order to manage a negotiating meeting effectively you will need to be skilful in how you establish *first* what is *not* negotiable. Then try to reach a WIN-WIN resolution.

What you call your meeting is not important, but what

people expect from a meeting *is* important. A close friend and trainer said, 'I went to the wrong meeting for ten years...' The people on the course on which he said this looked amazed, but then understood as he went on to explain 'I thought I was going to a collegiate meeting, but my senior manager was running a command meeting.' Hence his needs were not met, and frustration set in.

So what names do you give to your meeting and also, I wonder, what names do your staff use to describe those you hold? 'The blood bath'? 'The weekly wail'? 'The monthly motivator'? or the 'Exciting encounter'? Perhaps you could ask them at your next meeting.

The word 'meeting' implies for most a group of people, but you are having a meeting even when you are with one other person. How you behave in that setting is also important.

How do I manage meetings successfully?

In order to develop your management skills in meetings as a first-time or long-time manager you will have to manage new meetings regularly. To be EFFECTIVE you need to:

1   **Look** after your staff's comfort. Ensure that arrangements for coffee or refreshments and the room have been organized and confirm the time. You could delegate this to someone else, your secretary or a colleague. However, you are ultimately held responsible if things go wrong, even when you think it is not your job.

2   **Explore** the needs of your staff. Ask what are their expectations and needs from the meeting. You cannot do this individually if you have large numbers to manage.

3 **Arrive early** at the meeting. Turn up ten minutes before the allotted time and welcome everyone as they arrive.

4 **Decide to start the meeting on time**, even if stragglers come in late. Staff who come on time become irritated if you don't start on time. They made the effort and should not be expected to wait for disorganized people.

5 **Explain the purpose of the meeting** and ask if there are any other points that people need to raise at the beginning. This way late-comers will have missed their chance and hopefully will be on time for your next meeting. If someone is consistently late, you need to have a private word with them and ask them to be on time.

6 **Read your papers in advance**. Have the necessary papers at hand, having made notes on them. This clears your thinking and creates a sense of good leadership. Never read them through for the first time at the meeting.

7 **Stick to your time schedule** as far as possible for each item and finish within the allotted time. Most of your staff are busy people and will feel irritated if they cannot get to their next appointment punctually. They may leave courteously but resent being excluded from a missed part of the meeting.

8 **Handle emotions, hidden agendas** and address conflict as it arises, otherwise staff will leave feeling frustrated, angry or thinking the meeting was a waste of time.

9 **Involve everybody.** Ask people what they think has been decided. Do this frequently, especially if you think someone is there physically but not mentally. If your staff experience your asking them about their feelings or thoughts, they are more likely to be involved. You have

to deal with their responses, so if you are after a quiet life as a manager you will probably be ineffective as a manager of meetings.

10 **Prepare your staff** for action by checking out with each member (unless it is a public meeting and has more than ten members) what they believe they have to go away and do on leaving the meeting.

Here is a useful reminder:

L	Look after your staff's comfort
E	Explore the needs of your staff
A	Arrive early
D	Decide to start on time
E	Explain the purpose of the meeting
R	Read papers in advance
S	Stick to your time-schedule
H	Handle emotions
I	Involve everybody
P	Prepare your staff for action

If, however, you believe that managing a meeting successfully means being EFFICIENT rather than EFFECTIVE then you need to consider the following points:

1 Always indicate at the start of the meeting, the time the meeting will finish, and stick to it rigidly, even if there is still unfinished business. People will soon get used to the idea that they have got to get everything done in the time stated.

first time MANAGER

2   Do not turn up for a meeting more then ten minutes early. If you do, you could be spending your time more usefully somewhere else. But never be late.

3   Start the meeting exactly on time, whoever is not yet there. People will soon learn that if they arrive late they walk into a meeting in session.

4   If the meeting is a formal one, have spare copies of agendas, minutes and papers available. Some members always forget to bring them.

5   If the meeting is intended to be short, say less than 15 minutes, stay standing up. Once people sit down there is a tendency to settle into a long discourse.

6   If you are the chairperson, keep members rigidly to the agenda. Do not allow any member to introduce a new matter.

7   Never have A.O.B. on any agenda.

8   If a member of staff wishes to raise a matter for the agenda, either for a formal or informal meeting, have an agreed number of days' notice before the meeting for submission of the item.

9   Never discuss at length in a meeting something that can be more appropriately given to a member or working party to investigate and report back on.

10 Set meetings at a time that encourages people to be speedy. For example, hold them at 11.45 a.m., with lunch as the terminal time, or stack different meetings one after the other at hourly intervals. Friday afternoons seem to hurry people along.

Finally, I hope you prefer to be an *effective* rather than an *efficient* team manager. If you can do both, congratulations.

What kind of manager am I in meetings?

How do you manage yourself in meetings? Look at the following ten types of meetings and write down what you would say, or feel, or do, if you were in such a meeting as a member of that group.

How can I manage the following ten situations in meetings as a MEMBER of that meeting. Write your brief answers under each given situation.

1 The dictator

An unresponsive meeting

_____

_____

_____

_____

2 The socially inept

An unsociable meeting

_____

_____

_____

_____

3 The unprepared

A stilted meeting

_____

_____

_____

_____

4 The blamer

A scapegoat meeting

_____

_____

_____

_____

5 The gruesome twosome

A tête-à-tête meeting

_____

_____

_____

_____

6 The them and us

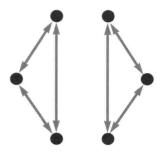

A 'them and us' meeting

_____

_____

_____

_____

7 The excluder

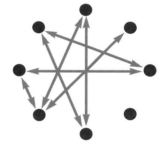

An isolating meeting

_____

_____

_____

_____

8 The raging bull

A conflict between two
angry colleagues

_____

_____

_____

_____

9 The information giver

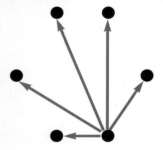

A dominant leader meeting

_____

_____

_____

_____

10 The separatist

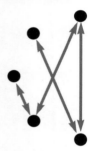

A cliquish meeting, usually about status

_____

_____

_____

_____

Which of the ten types of manager of meetings do you tend to be. If you are not sure ask your staff.

Tick the one you think you are for future reference and to see if you have changed after reading this book.

The dictator	☐	The divider	☐
The socially inept	☐	The excluder	☐
The unprepared	☐	The raging bull	☐
The blamer	☐	The information giver	☐
The gruesome twosome	☐	The separatist	☐

The skilled manager

Remember this is the ideal. If you are a successful manager, you will aim for the ideal.

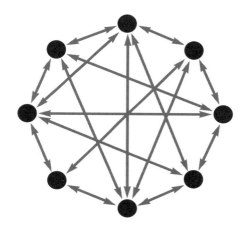

Am I formal, frustrating, or fun?

As a first-time or long-time manager you may be anxious about getting the balance right, achieving your goals but also working to maintain good relationships. Try to recognize the power of balance in your meetings. You may decide to alternate your meetings, one week a formal information-giving session, followed by an open meeting, where staff choose the agenda and talk about their perceptions.

Imagine that you are sent an agenda on which are the following items:

1 Staffing
2 Quality
3 Expenses

■ What is going through your mind?

Item 1 'Will be about cutting back on staff', but another person may see that as more about staff appointments because that is what they perceive as important.

Item 2 'Yes, that will be about the quality control report I wrote', but another person may envisage that the item is about the fact that the quality of their product needs improving.

Item 3 'Someone must have been fiddling their expenses claim form', but another person may think that company cars are now to be implemented to save on personal petrol expenses. It could be anything when the item is so woolly and general.

Write your agenda so that people know what it is about, which also gives staff time to think or talk about the issues. Also, put an approximate time to items so that you are informing them of its time-value. Some staff may only need to come in for certain items, so they need some time guideline. For example:

1	Staffing	New appointment requests	20 minutes
2	Quality	Report from ... Department X	10 minutes
3	Expenses	New forms	5 minutes.

Then you have the Minutes. If you are a formal manager, you are likely to want them lengthy and in detail. But this is a waste of time. Minutes are primarily to check progress, so be concise and put *who* is to take the action. Otherwise you will end up with 'somebody said they would do something about this but nobody has'.

◼ Frustration – what causes it at meetings?

Here are a few possible suggestions to put it right:

1 Sit where you can see and hear everybody. People who sit facing the chairperson or power person are usually vying for power or simply want to be seen.

2 Arrange chairs in positions of equal importance and always get rid of the 'death chair'. The empty chair can mean that some people will feel subconsciously frustrated that they have bothered to turn up but 'it' has not.

3 If you feel frustrated by someone waffling, then say so. 'That sounds important, please discuss that with ... and give me your recommendations'.

4 Give solutions, not problems.

5 If you think it – say it. There is little point in thinking something but not saying anything because you are worrying about the fact that others may believe that you are stupid. If you don't say it, someone else might, and then they get the praise. You end up feeling frustrated because you thought of that idea ten minutes earlier.

6 Empower yourself with your language. If you are feeling frustrated, say so. 'I feel frustrated when you ...' Do not give your power away by saying 'You make me feel frustrated when ...'

7 Watch your body language. Avoid folding arms, pointing fingers, looking away when people are speaking: all these postures can cause a great deal of frustration in others.

8 Rotate the role of the chairperson. You probably behave differently when you are chairing a meeting from when you are a member of a group. This gives you and others the

opportunity to show how you would organize things and avoid frustration, certainly for yourself, if not for others.

9 Ask how people are feeling. This is one of the most difficult things to do, especially if you avoid managing conflict in meetings, or anywhere else. Say how you are feeling if you hear 'frustrated', then ask 'What is that about?' Do not ask 'Why?' since that can sound intimidating.

10 Check that everybody understands what is expected of them after the meeting. This avoids frustration, especially if they have to do something that isn't their job. Think who, when, how, and ensure they know why it is to be done. Understanding why they have to do something helps people to behave more positively.

Have some fun!

1 Humour is a great stress releaser. Use it.

2 Give permission for jest.

3 Laugh with colleagues – not at them.

4 Ask people what they think ... is likely to say.

5 Have bondability – look for what you share, rather than how you differ.

6 Try brain-storming. Agree no discussion until all have contributed. Say 'anything goes'.

7 Ask what titles your staff would like if they could choose.

I cannot believe they appoin you – I should ha got your job!

You're so two-faced – have you forgotten what you told me confidentially?

I agree v you.

That s value for

I cannot believe you're paid the money you get.

Now they ar trustworth

I couldn't trust you an inch. I wonder who you trod on to get to your position.

8. Set some ground rules. Suggest fun being one of them.

9. Have ten minutes when you rule that nobody speaks unless they first say what the previous person has said.

You may like to try one or two of these tips at your next meeting. Or show the members the list and see what they think.

The meeting – what are they really thinking?

first time MANAGER

Study again the ten suggestions for making meetings less frustrating on pages 67 and 68. With experience you may be able to distinguish that the:

'formalist managers' will probably like suggestions 7, 8 and 10; Whereas the
'sociocentric managers' will lean towards 3,5 and 6, and the
'personalistic managers' will be attracted to 1, 2 and 4.

So expect some fun!

What might my staff think of me?

Do people say what they think? Not necessarily!

What they say to me may not be what they think of me. Listen to the music behind the words.

What is my management style?

So how do you manage meetings? Do you, as the chairperson, handle meetings in one of the four ways listed below? Briefly write down what you do to rectify the situation, if it should happen to you as the manager.

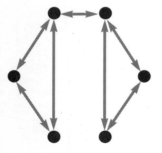

1 End up with a fragmented, cliquish meeting

_____

_____

_____

_____

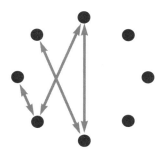

2 Allow an in-group/silent group to happen

_____

_____

_____

_____

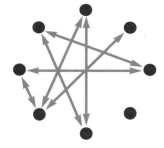

3 Allow yourself and others to isolate someone

_____

_____

_____

_____

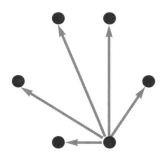

4 Make everybody address the chair so that you are the dominant leader – it becomes a question and answer session

_____

_____

_____

_____

My management style at meetings is:

_____

_____

_____

_____

_____

_____

I have the following skills in managing meetings effectively. The skills that I need to work on are:

_____

_____

_____

_____

_____

_____

CHAPTER 5

How can I successfully use my time?

Can I plan for certain scenarios?

Do you make excuses when people mention how you could use your time more productively? For instance, do you say 'I like to act spontaneously'? Planning for being spontaneous is a contradiction in terms, but without planning you will have little opportunity to be spontaneous. You can always plan for time to do nothing.

Or perhaps you say, 'What is so good about saving time? I like to take things as they come'. You will have more time to take things as they come if you plan to get jobs done that have to be done. Planning should lead to your being more organized and confident in your role as manager, ultimately allowing you more time for pleasure, spontaneity and relaxation. So now try to plan how you could use your time more wisely in the following potentially time-wasting scenarios.

1	Making meetings more productive
2	Conquering procrastination
3	Filling the time gaps between tasks
4	Coping with background reading
5	Dealing with wafflers

1 Making meetings more productive

Tomorrow afternoon you are due at a meeting to be chaired by your line manager and attended by half a dozen of your colleagues of both genders, three of whom are of equal seniority and three of whom are more junior than yourself. The meeting is not a formal committee and no one acts as secretary. You anticipate it with a sinking feeling. The meetings are always a total shambles with no clear agenda and invariably take far more time than is justified.

You really feel you must do something about the effectiveness of these regular meetings. The problem is you are not in the chair and are unable to tell your line manager about his/her lack of skills, Everyone, however, is so frustrated that something must be done, but what?

2 Conquering procrastination

Four weeks ago you were asked to undertake the production of a report for consideration at a meeting of a key committee which takes place in three weeks' time. The report will require 6–8 sides of A4 to do the topic justice. You already have a pretty good idea of the key issues that the report will need to cover, but do not have all the supporting and background information immediately to hand. When you were first asked to do the report, the meeting of the committee seemed a long time away and now only two weeks remain before the papers for the meeting need to be circulated. You know you will need at least a day to write the report but the normal flow of work, including the endless interruptions, just won't give you a chance to get on with it. At least three days will be required for typing and printing the report. What should you do to make sure it is produced on time?

3 Filling the time gaps

Your disposition is such that you have no difficulty in settling down to a solid morning's work at your desk. However, some days seem to be punctuated by a series of meetings with a number of short gaps between them – time that you find difficult to use productively. You tend to return to your desk after one appointment and find it difficult to use the gap before the next. You always like to be in good time for an appointment and at the same time you find it frustrating that you have to waste five or ten minutes if a meeting or appointment starts late. What should you do to use this time more effectively?

4 Coping with background reading

There are a large number of reports and periodicals which it is important that you should read in order to have the necessary background information to do your work effectively. Many of these are passed around on a circulation list and somehow a mass always seems to come in just at the time when you are busiest. You have a tray in your office into which you put material which should be read as and when you are able, and it just seems to pile up. Because it is never really urgent, somehow it stays and gets neglected. You feel there should be a better way of managing this task, but how?

5 Dealing with wafflers

There are a number of your colleagues, including some staff for whom you have a responsibility, who always take a dozen words to say something that could be said in one. Two people in particular you dread meeting. You never seem to be able to get away in less than fifteen minutes and you always feel frustrated at wasting so much of your time. Somehow you just don't feel you can get away without being rude. However, you feel you must evolve some sort of strategy to avoid wasting so much time, but what is it to be?

Do my internal messages affect how I use my time?

Work habits and their effect on time structuring

In Chapter 2 you were able to recognize if your 'behaviour' affected how you related to other people. Now see if it affects your work habits.

As discussed earlier, we all have certain internal messages, sometimes called 'monkeys (or creatures) on the shoulder' or 'drivers', which dictate how we respond psychologically to the many different situations we find ourselves coping with every day at work. These 'monkeys' or 'drivers' can be sorted into five categories which broadly influence the way in which we respond to any given situation. They are: Be perfect, Please others, Hurry up, Be strong and Try harder.

Let us take a look at how these internal messages might affect different people in terms of how they use their time.

Be perfect

If you have a Be perfect driver you are the sort of person who completes a task so that it will not need to be redone. You are probably very well organized and you can probably find things easily because you plan carefully and methodically.

However, the disadvantage is that you might spend too much time doing the perfect job, which possibly may not need the amount of analysis and the perfection you adopt, or the amount of time which you allocate to it. You probably explain more than is necessary. You could over-plan or you could make projects longer by constantly checking and rechecking.

Please others

If you have an internal message which says you must be nice to other people, then you lean over backwards to appease them and to meet their needs rather than your own. You are very good at creating harmony and you definitely save time for other people. However, you may save other people's time by losing your own. Allow others to eat into their own time. Your disadvantage is that you are so eager to please everyone else that you forget to take time for yourself. Probably your time is wasted by answering too many unnecessary questions and attending too many unnecessary consultations.

Hurry up

The advantage of this particular monkey is that you do produce a lot of work in a short time and you are probably excellent on jobs that do not require vast amounts of intricate detail. However, you probably hurry up through important work, missing details, and it is highly likely that you frequently get work returned to do over again. Maybe you do not take enough time to explain to other staff and colleagues what is actually needed from them, making assumptions and mistakes in your hurry to get them started on the next task, which will also, of course, cost you time in the long run.

Be strong

You probably make balanced, rational decisions that are free from emotion because you do not like sharing your feelings with other people. Your personality may be such that you are not bothered too much about what your staff think of you, and as a consequence you are probably freer from interruptions by people, than your colleagues. You make it known that you can manage your job perfectly well without any help whatsoever and that you do not take kindly to being interrupted. The disadvantage of the Be strong driver is that you are probably poor with human relationships. Staff may hesitate about approaching you for whatever reason. This may cause problems that will eventually eat up your time, as well as the time of the whole office, because you have not dealt with, or even been aware of, difficulties when they first arose.

Try harder

The advantage of your trying harder is that you probably accomplish tasks well, even if you do not do them as quickly as others. One of the disadvantages is that you do not take short cuts and you make decisions too slowly. You may not take any risks for fear of failing. You are probably wasting time by thinking abut how you could do this better if you tried harder.

What are the questions that you need to ask yourself?

If you are trying to be perfect you need to ask yourself 'What am I spending my time on that does not require first-class perfection and performance?'

If you are into pleasing others you need to ask yourself, 'What must I accomplish today for ME even if I do not do anything for anyone else. How can I please MYSELF as well as others?'

If you are into hurrying up then you need to ask yourself, 'What tasks need my fullest attention and when in the day can I plan to do them so that I will not need to rush them?'

If you are into being strong, you should ask yourself, 'If I were more open with my staff, what would really happen? Does my fearful fantasy really have any substantial foundation? Perhaps I could sometimes admit that I am having difficulty with certain aspects of my work'.

If you are into trying harder you need to ask yourself, 'Is it really that hard? What shortcuts could I take in order to accomplish jobs more quickly?'

■ Structure some 'selfish time' for yourself

Managing time effectively is another way of reducing your stress.

Time structuring

Complete the pie charts overleaf with the time you spend in *one day* and *one week* on work, family, hobbies, housework, as a mother/father, sister/brother, daughter/son, wife/husband /partner, friend and on yourself. It is important to give yourself some 'selfish time'.

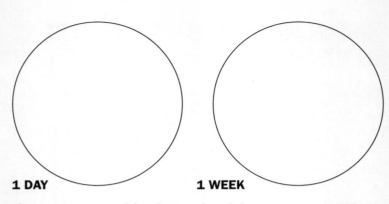

1 DAY **1 WEEK**

If you are surprised by the results of this exercise, would you like to make any changes? How would you like to have this 'pie of time'?

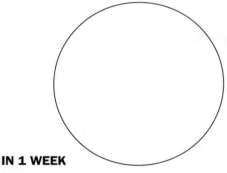

IN 1 WEEK

What are you going to do in order to achieve these changes?

_____

_____

_____

_____

_____

_____

_____

100 ways to save time

■ Personal needs and reasons for saving time

1　Think about what you want to do with the time that you save.

2　Decide on the real purpose of your life and your career. Do you live to work or work to live?

3　Break down your goals into attainable targets.

4　Everything you do should contribute to your saving time in order to enjoy the time that you have saved.

5　Always ask yourself, 'Is what I'm doing right now moving me forward towards a work or life goal?' If not, don't do it, or think 'How can I make the best use of my time right now?'

■ Personal planning

6　Plan your time: don't let it control you. Blank in 'if only' days in the diary – 'if only I had the time I'd …' – then you could gain time to do the things you want to.

7　Try to prioritize your work. Allocate priorities to projects, tasks, in-tray, post, and so on. Priorities are either urgent or important: make your choice – although some things could be both urgent and important.

8　Paper time-saving: Arrange and allocate priorities and categories to your paper, memos, etc: A (urgent, important); B (not sure); C (pending) and D (bin it).

9　Throw away the Ds. Some of you may find it difficult to throw things away, but remember if it is really important, usually someone will have a copy.

10 Rearrange Bs (not sure about) into either the A or C pile.

11 Keep the Cs to be read during non-priority time. Put them in a drawer. Do not have a 'pending' tray. Remember though, **your** C pile might be someone else's A pile.

12 Sub-prioritize your A pile – A1, A2, A3, etc.

A1 – what you do not like to do

A2 – difficult but may be able to do

A3 – easy

13 Do the A1s **now**, then your other As (not those attractive Cs, that you could just sit and read.)

14 Make appointments with yourself in your diary – this is the personal time you must have during the day. Lunch, seeing someone who motivates, excites or supervises you.

15 Stick to your plan – make it and do it now. Once you start something, finish it, if possible. If it's too large, divide and conquer manageable pieces – the 'Swiss cheese' approach. Go for small parts of a job or project even if you cannot complete the task in hand.

16 Plan your weekends, if only to do nothing but relax.

17 Select your personal and work 'best' times to get things done, and plan to do your most important work then. Some people find the morning, midday or evening a time more conducive to work.

18 Estimate the time for a task, not just the starting time, but how long it will take. Set and keep to deadlines for each task. If the job is more complex, then give yourself intermediate deadlines.

▌ Daily operating

19 Use the 'To-do' system. Have a daily 'To-do' list –
    particularly for your A items.

20 Review your daily list either first thing in the morning or
    last thing in the evening and plan your priorities. Do this
    by numbering each item as to the ones you need to
    complete first. Keep your daily 'To-do' list always in
    sight.

21 As you clear each item, delete it in brilliant red – just
    looking at a list of completed tasks makes you feel
    better! But don't include too many items.

22 Write it down – don't try to keep your 'To-do' lists in
    your head – keep that free actually to do.

23 Use the 'To-do' lists – don't ignore them. They are
    probably your most powerful time-management tools.
    Remember to do the things you don't like doing first.

24 Have the things you need constantly together in one
    place, close to hand.

25 Clear your desk and tidy out your drawers. Be ruthless;
    save time by dumping rubbish you have not used in ages.
    Be sure to clear your desk at the end of every day.

26 Interruptions are probably what you're paid to do. If they
    are, accept them. If they aren't, stop them.

27 Ask yourself, 'What can I do in order to take some short
    cuts?'

28 Strive to do the best you can. Total excellence or
    perfection is unattainable. Whereas doing the best you
    can is healthy, perfection is impossible, frustrating and a
    waste of time.

Personal delegation

29 Delegate whenever possible – downwards, sideways, upwards.

30 Delegate tasks but do not abdicate them – if it is your task, you still have the final responsibility.

31 When delegating, delegate the power with the job and support any decisions that are made by the person to whom you delegated.

32 Don't keep poking your nose in at times, to make sure the person is doing it, when you haven't agreed to do so.

33 Always make the instructions for the tasks you delegate complete and clear and ensure that they have been understood.

34 Always give or agree a final completion date.

35 Find new tasks and new ways to delegate – this saves your time and develops your staff.

36 Arrange for decisions to be made at the lowest realistic level.

Making meetings effective

37 To conduct effective meetings, first decide whether they are necessary and do not have them just because it is 'Monday'.

38 Allocate both starting times and finishing times wherever possible and stick to them.

39 Ask yourself, 'Do I want a meeting for information-giving or is it the process and hidden agendas that I need to explore?' Alternate meetings, one to gain information, two to have an open agenda.

40 Making your agenda mean something – don't just have a 'shopping list' which does not tell the members whether they are to discuss, to decide, to recommend, etc. Write your agendas for meetings as questions you want answered. When possible add a name as to who will lead the debate. Give an approximate time, for example, fifteen minutes for some items.

41 Whenever possible, go to just the part of the meeting that is relevant to you.

42 Are the right people at the meeting?

43 Is everything necessary to the meeting there and have all the relevant papers been sent out beforehand? Do not waste time reading them at the meeting.

44 What are the other people's issues likely to be?

45 If someone is talking on and on about a certain issue, suggest to them that he or she writes you a memo or paper, or discusses that issue with you over coffee later; say that, if necessary, you will bring it back to the full meeting.

46 Go to the other person's room to meet them – you can always get up and go.

47 Stay standing up when you have a meeting with somebody if your time is short.

48 If you have an agenda spot in somebody else's meeting, try to obtain a definite time for it.

first time MANAGER

Telephone control

49 Plan your telephone calls – use telephone 'To-do' lists. Use a pad rather than a separate piece of paper. This way you have a record of what you have done.

50 Horsetrade telephone reception with a colleague when you want some uninterrupted time.

51 If someone is not available and you have to leave a message, then if possible arrange a specific 'call back' time – don't just say 'I'll ring you later' or even worse 'You ring me later'.

52 Leave messages on answer phones, do not avoid speaking to them. At least the ball is then in the other person's court.

53 Have your call-interceptor briefed to record name, company, number and extension, reason for call and convenient time to ring back.

54 Give your call-interceptor authority to make certain decisions on certain subjects on your behalf, such as a suitable call back time.

55 If interrupted during a task like writing, before answering the call, pencil in your next thoughts. When you return to your task you will know what you were thinking or writing about before the telephone interruption.

56 Cross-index your telephone directory – names as one entry, organization as the other entry.

57 Quickly get to the point and purpose of the call – it's pleasant to socialize or gossip, but it wastes a lot of time.

58 Make sure that you get the call-back name and/or number right – it's better to ask for the information until you have got it right, rather than lose the information.

59 Be in control of your telephone, you don't always have to answer it.

60 If someone is engaged, press 5 – that way they will return your call when they have finished – rather than waste time by keeping on ringing them. Not all telephones can accept this instruction, but try it.

Personal discipline

61 Time management is 99 per cent self-discipline.

62 Recall your purpose, aims and objectives – do you really want to achieve them?

63 STOP working at trying to please people all the time, try to learn to say 'NO'.

64 Try to do it right the first time – every time you have to try again, you are wasting time.

65 How open is your 'open door'? Should it be as wide open as it is? Close it sometimes so that you can get on with work that you want to do.

66 Use a 'Do not disturb' notice.

67 Avoid procrastination – get on with it.

68 Identify your time-wasters and avoid them where possible.

69 Set yourself personal deadlines for most tasks and stick to them if at all possible.

70 Stick at the task you know must be done.

71 Do one thing at a time. Stay focused.

72 Always have something to do – even if it is constructive relaxation.

73 Always be on time yourself. Arrive at meetings 10 minutes beforehand. It is psychologically empowering.

74 Use stress-reduction techniques.

75 Learn from previous mistakes so that you can devise ways of preventing a repetition.

Paper

76 Handle a piece of paper only once.

77 The only reason for taking home your briefcase is to bring tomorrow's lunch to work.

78 If you can't deal with it once you've picked it up, note it on your 'To-do' pad and put it away.

79 If possible, use a dictating machine or computer rather than script drafts.

80 Set up a system to bring things up automatically on specific dates.

81 Use routine letters or paragraphs for as much correspondence as possible.

82 Memos are only for announcing, confirming, clarifying, reminding. They are not for dialogue, it is better to speak.

83 With regard to files, ask yourself the following questions:

   — What's the worst thing that could happen if this file didn't exist?

   — Am I the only person who has this information?

   — Do I really need this information?

84 Usually you can throw most of them away. A few fat files are better than a lot of thin ones. If a file hasn't been used for a year, then throw it away. If in doubt, throw it out.

85 If it is really important, someone else will have a copy.

◼ Reading

86 Read only what you must. Read the summaries of reports.

87 Try to increase your reading speed.

88 Learn how to scan important items.

◼ Travelling

89 Leave in plenty of time to arrive for appointments. If early, you can use your time to read or relax.

90 Don't be a one-side-of-the-town-to-the-other traveller – plan groups of visits within easy reach of each other.

91 Use car cassette learning or relax with talking books on long journeys.

92 Keep a Dictaphone close at hand for any ideas on things you need to remember.

93 Use travel time as speech rehearsal time. Talk out loud, don't just think about the speech.

94 Consider having a car phone, preferably outward calls only. Remember it is illegal to drive and use a mobile phone.

95 Use train journeys to read, write, discuss and to brainstorm ideas on your own or with the colleagues travelling with you.

96 If you cannot get to sleep, then read rather than worry about it.

97 Make lists for shopping.

98 If you have an expense or travel account, keep a small pad in your car, briefcase or bag, and put down the cost as you pay for such things or note how many miles you have travelled for your expense claim form.

99 Go for small successes, not big failures.

100 If you always do what you've always done — you'll always get what you've always got. So try something different — it may save you time.

CHAPTER **6**

How can I be successful and cope with pressure at work?

How can I relate better to people at work?

To feel positive at work and gain a feeling of joyfulness, fulfilment or success, you will need to relate to people in an honest, genuine way. Now I will focus on how you can relate more positively to your colleagues and managers.

One golden rule is to be open. Say what you want to say, ask for what you need, but be prepared to listen to the other person's point of view.

There may be times at work when you feel frustrated because you are not getting what you want, so ask or tell the person concerned how you feel. At other times you may feel angry or upset about what someone has said or done to you. Address the conflict, tell them what has annoyed or upset you, what you have observed, and how it makes you feel and what you need.

In such instances, watch your language. Saying 'You make me feel angry when ...' gives the other person the power. Instead, try saying 'I feel angry when you ...' That gives you the power. Other people don't make us feel anything; we make ourselves feel positive or negative by the way in which we think about certain behaviour or conversations.

How to gain confidence

Assertiveness and self-confidence

In most situations you will think about what to do or say, or how to react, and your reactions will depend largely upon your past experiences and thoughts in similar situations or circumstances. The type of thoughts that you have previously experienced will trigger certain responses within you. Those negative or positive feelings then bring about your negative or positive behaviour.

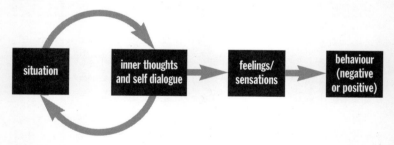

So how you think and what you feel affects how you behave. If you think a situation will be a positive experience, you will feel confident and your behaviour will therefore be positive and assertive.

Self-affirmations are positive, assertive statements that affirm a person's self-worth and self-confidence, for example 'I am an intelligent woman' or 'I am an intelligent man'. Affirmative self-talk tends to lead to assertive behaviour.

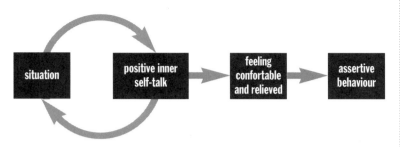

Now complete the following questionnaire to find out how assertive you are.

QUESTIONNAIRE 6
How assertive are you?

● ●

Complete the following questionnaire to identify aspects of your life in which you feel either assertive or non-assertive. Decide how confident you are in the following situations? Circle each statement 1, 2, or 3 to indicate your response.

1   I feel tense

2   I feel moderately OK

3   I feel fine

Your appearance

a)	Speaking in front of a group of people	1 2 3	
b)	Walking into a room of men/women	1 2 3	
c)	Keeping eye contact when addressing someone you like	1 2 3	

Your mind

a) Requesting service that is not forthcoming   1   2   3
in a shop, restaurant, travel agent, etc

b) Asking for feedback about your performance   1   2   3
in cooking, gardening, appearance, DIY

c) Being alone in a group of couples   1   2   3

Addressing conflict

a) Disagreeing with someone   1   2   3

b) Asking probing questions at a meeting or of   1   2   3
one of your family

c) Stating your differing views to a male/female   1   2   3
authority figure – doctor, lawyer, police,
manager, line manager

Saying no

a) Saying 'No' when asked to baby-sit, lend   1   2   3
money, or work overtime, when you
don't want to

b) Saying 'No' when asked to help in a   1   2   3
voluntary capacity for charity

c) Saying 'No' to giving someone a lift that is   1   2   3
out of your way

Establishing your values

a) Commenting about a racist or sexist remark   1   2   3
in a group

b) Addressing a put-down, such as: 'You're   1   2   3
intelligent for a woman', or 'You're
sensitive for a man'

c) Asking for 'thinking it over' time   1   2   3

Total   ☐ ☐ ☐

Scores for Questionnaire 6

15–20   You need to work on your assertive skills

20–30   In some situations you can be assertive, but look
             at the ones that cause you anxiety

30 plus   You are assertive, you have 'a life'

What are the differences between passive, assertive and aggressive behaviour?

	Passive	Assertive	Aggressive
Voice	quiet	clearly audible	loud
Language	unsure, indirect, 'might, maybe'	direct, concise, 'I want, need, have'	argumentative, accusative: 'should, will'
Eyes	lowered	straight gaze	glaring or expressionless
Body language	hunched, stooped, withdrawn	upright, shoulders down, open gestures	pointing finger, curled fists, hands on hips – fingers forward, chin forward, rigid, folded arms
Attitudes	'could do better', like to please, easily persuaded, my fault	'I know what I need', prepared to listen, to find out the needs of others	'Don't argue with me', think they are right, stubborn, fascist, racist
Feelings	fear, guilt, inadequacy, insecure, unsure	confident, self-love, calm, democratic	anger, frustration, revenge, autocratic. See themselves as superior
Early childhood messages	turn the other cheek, don't push yourself forward, be nice	as good as anyone else, you are special, you are loved	stand up for yourself, don't let anyone win, fight, hit back

What is assertiveness?

Assertiveness is being honest, open, direct, focused, and asking for what you want or need, while recognizing that others also have their needs.

What is passive behaviour?

Being passive is withholding true feelings, maybe trying to please others, feeling insecure or even anxious about your relationship, role or job.

What is aggressive behaviour?

When someone is aggressive, they are likely to be a bully, domineering, patronizing, stubborn and hostile, sometimes even violent, towards others. Such behaviour is often associated with racism or sexism.

What do you gain from being assertive?	self-love and self-confidence inner harmony quality of life real intimacy caring friends trust and respect influence improved relationships positive role model for children
What do you gain from being passive?	a quiet life avoid conflict control inner feelings praise for conforming
What do you lose by being passive?	the ability to clear the atmosphere of conflict the respect of others the power to make decisions the satisfaction of initiating and succeeding in relationships psychosomatic wellness (anger turned inwards, frozen anger, can lead to depression)

What other differences are there?

The voice, the language that is used, the eyes, body posture, attitudes, feelings, how people perceive themselves and their different early childhood messages.

Are you happy with your gains, or are the losses in your life greater? Would you give up some of the gains for the positive aspects of being assertive? Being assertive means that you know yourself as an emotional human being, and you are able to look after yourself.

Learning to be assertive

1   You may choose to start by realizing that you can say 'No'. Later you will learn to say 'No' without feeling guilty.
2   You are allowed to make mistakes, so admit them. You can use humour to deal with a critical situation by saying, 'That's the first mistake that I've made in my life.'
3   You can ask for what you want, recognizing that others have needs too. People cannot read your mind, so tell them what you are thinking or feeling.
4   The word 'I' gives you power. Say 'I need to think that over' or 'I feel hurt when you treat me in that way, *not* 'you make me feel hurt'. That's giving your power away to the other person.
5   Express your feelings. Avoid turning them inwards.
6   Accept yourself and give yourself permission to grieve or be angry or ill. Avoid trying to be wonder-woman or superman.

7   Use assertive language.
    'I wish to say. . .'
    'I believe. . .'
    'I think. . .'
    'I feel. . .'
    'I need to. . .'
    not
    'Can I just say. . .?'
    'Can I add to what you have just said'
    It sounds like permission-seeking, like asking 'Can I just
    have a little breath of your air?'

8   Look after yourself emotionally, physically and mentally.
    Take selfish time and enjoy it. Treat yourself to small
    luxuries, rebuild your self-esteem. Take exercise, relax,
    stand upright, eat sensibly.

9   Smile when you want to, not because you think you have
    to so that people will like you.
    Powerful people smile when pleased.
    Powerless people smile to please.

10 Open up your body, maintain an accepting eye contact.
    Lower shoulders and hold head and spine upright.

Coping with criticism

How do you react to criticism? Some people start to justify
their behaviour while others say nothing but feel angry or
upset. Others respond by blaming someone else.

Think of an example when someone has criticized you.

1   What exactly did they say?
2   How did you respond?
3   What was the outcome?

Now ask yourself …

4   Was the criticism valid or invalid?

5   If it was valid, did you agree with it?

6   If it was invalid, did you disagree with it and say why it was invalid?

7   Was the criticism vague?

8   Did you ask the other person to give you specific examples?

9   Who had the problem?

10 What could you do differently next time?

Analysis of criticism

When you are criticized, first ask yourself 'is this criticism valid or invalid?' If it is valid, agree; if invalid, say that you think it is invalid and say why. If people are vague, ask them to be specific. Sometimes the other person has the problem, not you, and you need to tell them that it is not your problem. Speak evenly, do not resort to sarcasm.

VALID	INVALID		
Agree	Say it's invalid	Ask for specific examples	Who's got the problem?
Apologize. This takes the heat out of the situation	And say why. Perhaps there is a misunderstanding	Vague criticism needs to be focused	Say 'I can see that is a problem for you'. *This should be the last resort, try the other suggestions first.*

How to criticize others assertively

1   Tell them what you have observed

2   Tell them how you feel

3   Say what you need

For example:

- What I have observed... (is that you shout when I try to discuss our relationship).
- That makes me feel... (rejected and frightened, or angry).
- What I need is... (for us to discuss calmly what we are going to do about our money problem).
- Say 'I' to empower yourself.
- Say 'I have observed' so that they know you have observed, not someone else.
- Say how you feel, because people cannot argue with how you feel, they can argue with how you think.
- Say what you need, otherwise you just go round in circles, moaning rather than resolving.

I'm OK you're OK

To be assertive you need to operate from the psychological state of 'I'm OK you're OK'.

I'm OK You're OK (assertive)	I'm OK You're not OK (aggressive)
I'm not OK You're OK (passive)	I'm not OK You're not OK (depressed, pathetic)

Psychosomatic wellness

Do you believe there is such a thing as psychosomatic illness? If you agree, then do you think the other side of the coin could well be psychosomatic wellness?

In order to feel successful at work you will need to feel and think positively. I am now going to suggest four ways in which you can feel successful, and therefore more joyful, at work. These four suggestions involve looking at your behaviour and your physical needs as well as your emotional and cognitive skills.

How you can behave

I have just looked at assertiveness and time-management as ways of minimizing your pressure at work. Now I am going to suggest that you also start to regard relaxation as being an integral part of your working day. Relaxation at work may seem a most inappropriate concept, but nonetheless it is vitally important if you want to function and behave efficiently. Of course, there will be times when you will need to work at speed and under pressure, but it is essential from time to time that you pull away from your work, take a coffee break, or maybe a lunch break, away from your desk and have some interaction with other people.

Also think about the possibility of talking things through with colleagues when there are difficulties and you are feeling under pressure. Actually voicing your concerns out loud can help you to get things into perspective, and it very often enables you to hear your own answers. Your behaviour will be advantageously affected if you try to plan ahead, and pace yourself.

Physical needs

Your environment can contribute to your pressure, or ease your pressure. If you have a desk that is very untidy, or if you work in a chaotic office or workplace, try actually organizing and tidying these areas and arranging things around you in a way that makes you feel positive. As you are spending so much time at work, make it attractive, make it comfortable. Recognize the importance to your well-being of adequate heating, comfortable seating, efficient lighting and plenty of working space that is appropriate for the tasks you have to carry out.

Emotional needs

Think about problem-solving, rather than letting things nag at you. Try to resolve the matter by dealing with either the issue or the people involved. Assess what you need to say and say it. Remember to listen to what other people have to say to you, rather than making assumptions.

Set yourself small goals. Go for small successes rather than big failures. Be confident about your decisions. Remember, one in ten decisions is wrong and decisions can always be changed on experience and reflection.

Try to address conflict rather than withdraw, get angry, or just try to please people at your own emotional expense. Try to get things into perspective. Acknowledge that you may need to let go of some of your learned behaviour.

In order to feel well, and therefore happy, you will need to eat sensibly: your diet is important, as is some form of regular exercise.

Cognitive skills

How you think can affect how you behave and can affect how you feel, so try to think in a confident, positive way about your work. Celebrate your abilities and successes. Learn how to reframe, changing negative statements into positive statements, both from your own perspective and other people's way of speaking to you. Recognize your own limitations before you try to be excellent in everything.

◼ Emotional skills

Express how you feel. Ask for support when you need it and enjoy the company of your colleagues. Value other people's efforts and contributions to your daily work. Thank people, praise people, say 'Well done', and when people say similar things to you, say 'Thank you', rather than 'That's my job'. Above all, it's OK to laugh; it's OK to have a sense of humour; it's OK to have fun, just like it's OK to feel emotional and feel sexual, but it is important what you do with those feelings. Fear of embarrassment can spoil relationships and prevent people from feeling joyful. So take a risk! Don't hold back just because you might be embarrassed if they say yes or no to a request. Give yourself permission to have some fun!

CONCLUSION

■ People

By now you have probably recognized that there are several
barriers for you to overcome before you can begin to use
your time properly at work. It may be that you feel you are
badly managed or that your work is not properly planned.
Possibly meetings take up too much of your time, making tea
and coffee for people, or having non-work-related interruptions. Possibly you find it difficult to deal with people in
terms of communicating with them, or saying no to some of
the requests that are made of you. It is really important that
you decide upon what jobs have to be done before you think
about what you should, and ought, to be doing.

Focus upon how you are spending your time. Have you
discovered that you spend little time on personal maintenance
and too much time on other people? Perhaps some people
take up more of your time than others. Pirato, an Italian
philosopher, worked out the 'one-fifth – four-fifths' model.
Maybe you spend 80 per cent of your time on 20 per cent of
your staff? Just think about that! Are some of the staff with
whom you are working consuming a disproportionate amount
of your time?

Learn to be assertive. Don't waste time by beating about the bush; consider how you can ask for exactly what you want, remembering that you need to listen carefully to what the other person wants, too, before deciding how to press ahead.

If you do not understand what people are asking of you, ask them. Avoid wasting your time doing unnecessary jobs because you have been too concerned about looking stupid or inefficient to say, 'I don't understand'. You will probably be thought of more highly if you are prepared to say 'Hang on, I need you to explain that again'. Avoid procrastination: DO IT!

Think about scenarios that you have already worked on and consider whether in some way these experiences can help you to solve problems or situations with which you are currently having difficulties.

In terms of meetings, remember to send out agendas three days beforehand with lots of details on the agenda items, not just one-worders, and add an approximate time to indicate how long you are expecting each item to take. Make your Minutes as short as possible, concentrating on what action is to be taken rather than lengthy detail about what took place. Remember, at the end of each meeting, always check out with everyone there what they think they now have to do as a result of the meeting.

Paper

The golden rule is, handle a piece of paper only once where-ever possible. One little trick is that every time you pick up the same piece of paper and do nothing with it, tear a bit off the bottom of it and gradually the paper will disappear.

If you have been away from your desk for some time, you may have quite a pile of paperwork to deal with. First of all, sort it out into four piles: A Urgent or Important; B Cannot

Really Decide; C What you would normally call 'Pending'; D The Bin!. Then put your B pile either into A or C. A is for Action. These papers have some time element attached to them, and are urgent. The decision to categorize them as urgent, is, of course, based on your own value systems and beliefs. Sometimes people class things as important because of the identity of the person who is writing to them, or because the content of the memo, letter or report has a personal appeal.

Put C papers into a drawer. Remember that your C pile could be someone else's A pile.

Now working through your A pile, write on and take action on each piece of paper and pass to your secretary if you have one, with a short note to say 'answer this in the affirmative' for example. Avoid writing out long explanations – allow your secretary to create his/her own letter or memo.

Consider how you file your paper. You have probably got vast amounts of waste paper in your filing system. Whatever system you use, clear it out. Remember, if a piece of paper is really important, somebody will have a copy of it. You may say that you are the very person who needs to keep the copy, but you will have to decide that for yourself. More often than not there is a tremendous duplication of paper in workplaces. Some people choose to file alphabetically while others file by subject. Some people believe that one big file is better than lots of little ones.

One thought is to have a 'bring forward' system so that you file at the front things that need to be dealt with in the next month, and behind that things that need to be dealt with in the next twelve months. In this way you systematically bring forward the work that you are currently involved with. Put dates on your memos and papers. Again, you may decide to have a filing system that is in some kind of date order, depending upon your type of work.

Use a wall chart so you can see your diary at a glance. Choose a diary that offers you a page showing the year at a glance and mark it appropriately. Some people like to use IT packages for their diary on their computers, and others like to have the facility of going into other people's diaries – it is entirely up to you whether that is an appropriate way of working.

Save time by having a daily 'To-do' list and/or use your diary, both as a source of telephone numbers, meetings, conversations and memory joggers.

Have a 'To-do' system that works for you. Write your 'To-do' lists by prioritizing your jobs, trying to do the ones that you don't like doing first. Keep your 'To-do' list in one little book rather than having lots of bits of paper all over the place.

Pressure

You may have all kinds of pressures from the organization's expected work patterns, or your line manager or colleagues. If you are working in a long-hours culture, where you are expected to do overtime, you need to ensure that you organize yourself to keep a healthy balance between your work and your home life.

You can feel pressured by going to a photocopier that does not work or a coffee machine that is empty. Put idiot-proof instructions on equipment in order to avoid too many breakdowns owing to lack of knowledge or skill. Put a chair by the photocopying desk so that people can sit rather than having to stand. They may be able to use the time by reading what is coming off the photocopier or printer.

Use a 'Do not disturb' notice, or notes like 'Back at 3.30 p.m.' or similar. It has been suggested that when people working in the same office start to chat, anyone wishing not to be disturbed wears a distinctive kind of hat which is generally recognized as a 'I am busy and do not want to be disturbed' hat. A better way, however, would be to say 'I need to concentrate and your noise is disturbing me. Could you be quieter? Thank you!' Or find a quieter place to work.

Another way of reducing pressure might be to trade phone calls with a colleague, taking half-day sessions when you take their phone calls and they take yours. Try to work flexi-time since this can ease pressure when you need to deal with family or personal commitments. Sometimes, having a closed door prevents people constantly interrupting you.

If someone is asking you to do their work for them and they want you to give their work priority over yours, show them your 'To-do' list. Say to them 'Look, X is at the top of my list, that's urgent for so-and-so, if you negotiate with them, I'll put you at the top of my 'To-do' list.'

Finally, if you know that you like pleasing people, work on trying to please yourself first and getting your own work done before you have an open door policy to deal with everyone else's enquiries. Of course, your very job may be to do this, but you still need to look after yourself as well in order to avoid excessive pressure. Also, don't forget the importance of taking your lunchtime break. You will work smarter, not harder, by coming back refreshed to your desk or work area.

Remember that you can change your behaviour and that you are responsible for your own well-being and mental health. So take breaks, look after yourself in terms of diet, exercise and sufficient sleep. Request what you want and listen to what other people's needs are of you. Ask for support when you need it and talk through difficult aspects of your work with someone you can trust.

Think positively, celebrate your successes and ask for feedback about how you are doing. Thank other people for their efforts and good work. Accept 'warm fuzzies' (compliments) rather than discount them. Work towards small successes rather than big failures.

If you really want to be joyful and successful at work, you can be, but you may need to rethink some of your attitudes and change some of your behaviour. You will also need other people on whom you can lean from time to time, just as other people will need you.

The fact that you have bothered to read this book indicates that you are likely to be more successful and therefore enjoy your work as an effective manager.

The Civil List

Working habits are changing so quickly, no wonder I find it difficult to succeed!

Yes, they are, and you will need to change with them if you want to enjoy work and feel successful. To summarize, here are ten quick tips:

1 **Be flexible**
   Situations change and you will need to change with them.

2 **Be committed**
   Job commitment makes work so much more satisfying. It is therapeutic and an excellent antidote for stress.

3 **Accept uncertainty**
   If you knew everything was going to remain the same you would be bored. Uncertainty can give you the opportunity to change direction and try out new ways of working.

4 **Be a maker not a moaner**
   Stop playing psychological games and blaming others. Make things happen for yourself and your colleagues.

5 **Change your behaviour**
   Be assertive, not passive or aggressive. Be open, honest and genuine.

6 **Change your thinking**
   Look at your 'Drivers'. Knock some of those creatures that create inner self-talk, off your shoulders. 'Reframe' negative thinking.

7 **Make some selfish time**

'All work and no play ...' Create time in your life when you do something just for you. Enjoy your own company.

8 **Organize your working space**

Clear your desk. Bin the rubbish. Add things to your working area that please you.

9 **Take responsibility for yourself**

Say what you need and listen to what others need from you. Develop new skills. Take every opportunity for personal development.

10 **Have some fun**

Life is too short to be miserable. Ease up and give yourself permission to laugh.